Our World
In Verse

Laurie Wilkinson
The Psychy Poet

'Laurie crosses with ease from light and comical to deeply reflective and thought provoking in his own unique and accessible style'

Published in UK in 2021 by BadGoose Publishing.

Copyright © Laurie Wilkinson 2021

ISBN: 9798482731109

The right of Laurie Wilkinson to be identified as the author of this work has been asserted by him in accordance with the Copyright, Designs and Patents Act 1988.

Cover Photo: World in our Hands Sunset

Cover Design by: James Harvey.

All Best-Regards
Laurie

Introduction

Well here I am with another "bumper" book, now nine published in just over seven years. I am extremely happy with it and that said, each new book still surprises me a bit as I have now well exceeded my initial hopes and wildest dreams.

Since my eighth book was published in June 2020, the world has changed dramatically and in many ways for everybody and on a personal note, it changed a lot. My wife Iris, who suffered from dementia for some time, died in February 2021. During this time I continued to note my poem ideas, and many of those completed poems feature in this latest book.

In my last book I mentioned milestones and I continue with this theme and present my latest book as one of them. To clarify my milestones or achievements, they are largely my own feelings, wonderful compliments given, great reviews and an increased awareness of my work on several media settings.

Having had two poems in both The Daily Mail and then the Daily Mirror only last year (2020), further raising awareness and funds for the charity Help for Heroes that I have always donated to, I can say I am delighted with this success.

Apart from that, in the last 3 years I have had five of my poems read out live, and many more complimented about, on national radio, (that broadcasts internationally too), and I am now regularly asked to read my poems at many events. In the last couple of years I've also won two prestigious poetry competitions. I feel this all demonstrates the reasons for my increased confidence in my latest book, book nine!

This book follows my popular "tried and tested" format of romance, humour, reflection and tragedy that affect all our lives. Included are four themed articles and related poems that were published in the monthly column that I've been writing for The Sussex Newspaper Online for nearly 6 years now. AND for the very first time this latest book features eight poems with the stories behind the poems and how they came to be written.

There are also new poems about my created and still mischievous teddy bears "Ted and Beth" who are becoming increasingly popular and are of course included, alongside poems on our strange last year or so, and my experiences regarding this as well, I am sure you will recognise these, so I will leave you to explore it all.

This is an even bigger "bumper book" because not only does it have added new material as of my articles mentioned above and my usual multitude of brand new poems, but also a smattering of poems from across all of my books. For me. it's a celebration and demonstration of my growing poetic attributes and prolific poem production that I have the pleasure of bringing to you.

To help with this you will be aided by my popular comprehensive Appendix section to explain some not so obvious poems. I am confident that many of them will touch and resonate with you in some way as we again ride the roller coaster of our lives.

As ever, please enjoy this my ninth and latest book as "The Journey Continues"...

Laurie Wilkinson Bsc (hons) RMN

Acknowledgements

Well as this is now my ninth book I have finally realised, well a while ago actually, that it is almost impossible to recognise and acknowledge all the people and groups who have helped me, and that I will again to some extent repeat myself. Also no matter however long I make this, I will probably miss somebody out, and so for that and repeating myself I apologise now, but meanwhile I will do my best.

I do still need to recognise great and increased support and encouragement from family and friends, and especially my usual "supportive suspects" and also the various groups and organisations that I belong to.

So thanks again to the 42nd Highland Regiment (1815) re-enactment regiment, Anderida Writers Eastbourne, The Sussex Newspaper Online, that I write my monthly articles on, (for six years now). Local East Sussex businesses, shops, pubs, (many who sell my books), charities and all the wonderful people I meet and liaise with too numerous to mention individually by name, but I am grateful to.

I must continue to acknowledge a few special folks for their amazing support etc, so much gratitude to Elizabeth Wright (The Writer), who "guided and encouraged" me literally from my very start, Mick Seaman, and The Garden Bar Eastbourne Waterfront for their continued donations and support from my outset too!

Again the excellent Lynn Parsons of Magic National Radio must be thanked for all her fun, endorsements and mentions of me. Also now continuing the "Radio Theme", the sublime and lovely presenter of Radio Sussex & Surrey, Sylvie Blackmore who has kindly guested me on her show many times, and has a poem on her included inside under humour. Seb & Irene of Langney Tesco and team, and Nadia at Petra's "The Smugglers" pub Pevensey, who initiated idea of my "Sailor Bears" poem.

Oh, also my many friends in France, Lesley A T, a colleague from the past, Richard Williams for his advice, Geoff H a long ago school friend, Julie A V, Kelly Brown and family, Debbie & Sharon B's and Suanne Phillips still my fan from S. Africa, and Shona in New Zealand.

Many, many more must remain unmentioned but not forgotten as you will be thanked elsewhere and perhaps personally.....

James Harvey my excellent Website Guru is also publishing this book for me under Bad Goose Publishing as he did my eighth & previous book too, so a big thanks to him for all his help and guidance on this book and our new ideas, as I continue an increasingly prolific, determined and hopefully innovative poet and author!

As always my final recognition of gratitude is to you people taking the time to read this book, and with an even bigger thanks to the kind folks who have bought my previous books, and buy this one too, which as ever ensures my donation to the excellent charity Help for Heroes from all my sales.

Thanks again, and bless you all!

Our World in Verse

The world is our life's journey
Right up to our very last day,
However much we may not like it
Our times were made this way.

Now how we deal with fortunes
Will show the measure of us all,
Because in good or bad times
Some will stand and others fall.

So I note all these situations
But you might not see me look,
For descriptions of behaviours
Are now recorded in my book.

Contents

Laurie Wilkinson

ROMANCE

Laurie Wilkinson

Love and Trees

Maybe you'll never see how much I love you
Or possibly realise that you're so adored,
Because it may have all overpowered you
Making you complacent and perhaps bored.
For sometimes too much of a good thing
Can confuse and just seem like the norm,
But do not dismiss all that you receive
Freely given in every way and form.

Perhaps you take the trees for granted
With their magnificent spread and shade,
Forever constant in this glory of gifts
As if by angels they were all made.
For on many occasions in busy lives
Such statuesque wonder isn't seen,
Until arrival of sad or tranquil times
Awakens you to this sea of green.

Standing proudly tall or stretching wide
Poplars, willow, birch or imperial oak,
Nobly constant with liberal generosity
Of beautiful sights that they provoke,
In redundant minds and sad emotions
Confined to the mundane, or dire.
Before unleashing spectacles of delight
Causing a heart to soar much higher.

3

So the wonders now unseen or noted
Of unconditional love and adoration,
Could easily slip by sadly missed
If not aroused to an ecstatic elation.
Thus take a brief considering moment
And open your beautiful eyes to see,
How this priceless love is passing by
Offered wholly to you from me.

--ooOoo--

Awakening of Love

Love is defined as a great affection for,
And possibly a passionate attraction to
Your chosen muse, or centre of interest.
And mine is all focussed on you.

For you came out of the blue to me
At a time that I was quite unprepared,
To have any deep or inner feelings
So I guess I must have just stared,
At your photo and later in person
That seemed to take some time,
But it was definitely worth the wait
As you now say that you're mine.

Therefore excuse me just a little
If I seem to be all over the top,
Because I realise I'm lost to you
And It's not possible to just stop,
In my effusive words and thoughts
That I can only use to describe you,
And effects and emotions raised
Whenever I think about us two.

So please don't be overwhelmed
Or taken aback by how I feel,
Because although a surprise to me
I must confess that this is real.

Thus please indulge my affections
For I know that they are returned.
So when I accept I'm totally yours,
Not one bit of me is concerned.

--ooOoo--

Romance, Love or Lust?

A romance, love or even lust
Could really all mean the same,
But some aren't comfortable with this
So prefer to call it a softer name.
Now exactly what that would be
Depends on them or more their mood,
Because if too raunchy emotions felt
Could maybe make them sound rude.

For society likes to condemn others
On what they say and what they do,
Perhaps due to some jealousy felt ,
Which couldn't possibly be you?

For nobody likes to be left out
If others are having so much fun,
Especially a very lively sexual kind
They are losing and you have won.
So if you have a good relationship.
Of any depth or various type at all,
Please just indulge and enjoy it
For it drives some up the wall.

Now romance, love or lust feelings
Will so often take over our minds.
But many will perhaps deny them,
If they are the racy sexual kinds
Or inspirations and needs they have.
So may even retire to quietly play
As we all know tingling ideas lurk,
For they are felt by us every day.

Thus because it simply is very natural
And nature decrees we love this way,
That in life we are attracted to others
Hopefully with "little one's" some day.
So enjoy those fun and games needed
To get you to a very happy end,
For trying to deny or neglect them,
May drive you round the bend.

--ooOoo--

Autumn of Love

This poem is very nostalgic for me as it goes back to some of my earliest writing, and in this case a song that I wrote for one of the groups I sang with in the 60's. I had forgotten that I had written a few songs and quite a few lyrics back then, and until being reminded just after my prolific poem writing started from about 2012 onwards.

I have adapted this poem from one such song originally entitled "Autumn of our Love", so here it now is...

The autumn of our love is descending
No more to feel our heartbeats blending,
It's fading fast, the end it is near
Our love shares the fate of nature each year.

I never now see that spark in your eye
That was always there, however shy.
For I can tell that we're going wrong
Soon to be singing that saddest song.
That haunts all lovers that have lost,
Leaving us to count all the cost
Of wasted time, and broken dreams
Replaced by souls agony screams.

The autumn of our love is descending
No more to feel our heartbeats blending.
That loving magic is there no more
Laying instead nearly dead on the floor.

It never seemed to us we'd fail
To live forever in loves glow,
But people and times will always change
And turn into strangers you don't know.
So best to stand up, tall and square
With a new freshly painted smile,
That you know will see a lonely road
Hurting and aching, mile after mile.

Thus many a face will turn away
At your look of contagious gloom,
Whilst rushing back to lover or spouse
In a frantic bid to save their doom.

--ooOoo--

Laurie Wilkinson

Cut and Run

Just run away with me then
Drop it all and off we go,
To look at now and move forward
To feelings and places we don't know.

Come and leave it all behind
They are only possessions anyway.
For we can't take them with us
When we die those things all stay,
Alongside all that grief and woe
That we never did sign up for.
So that makes it so much easier
To just leave and shut the door.

Let us disappear hand in hand
Before we hear what people say,
For they won't ever understand us
Like Romeo and Juliet's of our day,
And unlike them we've seen life
So know how hard it can be.
Whilst they were besotted innocents
We are older, and must be free.

Oh I can hear the gossips scream
That we are selfish and just not fair,
But that is mostly a jealous cry
As to leave they wouldn't dare.

Then off we go my lovely siren
Away to see what will befall,
For we don't want a little sometimes
We want it now and must have it all.

And so now the deed is complete
There can be no going back.
We have eased our bodies together
Thus no sensations did we lack,
As our precious time we served
Doing all for the others sake.
But we know sadly it will be gone
When from our dream we will awake.

--ooOoo--

Foundation

If anything in life is going to succeed
A relationship, building or way of living,
It is imperative that it's all started well
From the bottom up and no leeway giving,
To allow any flaws or imperfections there
At this important statement of registration.
Because to last well and withstand assaults
It needs building on a strong foundation.

For most things in life will have their trials
Whether it is dwellings or relationships.
So we must take up our guard with this,
To ensure nothing precious to us slips
Away to be lost forever and maybe tainted,
Or perhaps has structurally dangerous flaws,
As we must protect what's precious to us
To prevent any sad closing of doors.

Although to build a reliable, sure feature
It takes great commitment and sacrifice,
For it must be durable and rock like
As great opportunities won't come twice.
So make your loving safe-haven secure
With much confidence in your creation,
That you can moor up to very happily
On getting to a desired life station.

But to complete this involvement well
It doesn't have to be all effort and toil,
Because you can have some enjoyment too
And good fun the industry won't spoil.
For with good chances of lasting content
You can just relax when you arrive,
Knowing with this strong foundation
Your love and creations will thrive.

--ooOoo--

Romantic Attraction (Article)

Dancing Light is originally from one of my monthly articles for an online newspaper, (that I have written for 6 years), which I have adapted and amended to nicely slot in here, I think, which describes romantic attraction, well in my humble opinion anyway.

Before I begin though, I want to post my disclaimer that I cannot be personally held responsible in any way for failed courtships or attempts to woo, trysts, broken hearts, or life changing upsets etc. These are (apparently?) all part of the alleged fun, intrigue, and general confusion of romance?

No not really for I am just being my usual sardonic self, so I will remind you of that old saying "it is far better to have loved and lost, than never to have loved at all". Yes, but really? Moving on quickly, let's have a look at attraction.

How do we think love and romance work on us with regard to attraction? In a very complex way is my answer. I certainly don't profess to know all, or perhaps much about any of this apart from being a biased and passionate poet maybe? However I do know from my own experiences and that of watching others, that attraction is very indiscriminate, for we are mostly all attracted to others at times, but somebody just "rings our bell" in a deeper way than anybody else. Not necessarily our dream person or photo fit, but just a person we seem to resonate with...

The first article poem on this subject, (written about twenty years ago), features in my very first book from 2014 called Poetic Views of Life.

Dancing Light

A dancing light to a room you are
Not seen at once but bright,
Your natural warmth is subtle too
Stronger still with frequent sight.

You are like the solid honest firs
That pretty flower to the moon,
Your laugh and fun could melt a stone
And cause sound minds to swoon.

I could be as your fantasy
Like a moth drawn to a lamp,
As others chase to be near you
Their joy tears running damp.

You may not know you radiate
This warm attracting haze,
Upon unsuspecting people met
Drawn in by your carefree gaze.

A dancing light to a room you are
That embraces all around,
To reach and skip in places dire
Where joy is seldom found.

--ooOoo--

A concern that our attraction or interest won't be recognised and returned is often a big fear. However, we must follow the scent and heed another old adage that "a faint heart never won fair lady (or man)", so off we go.

Maybe we can pick up signals that somebody is sending to us, but ho ho, I will not venture into that turmoil, for if and when those signals are confused, which of course can be very tricky, anything can happen, and often does! Quick another poem, and again from my first book.

Headlight

I have observed you much of late

You may have felt my looking stare,

Perhaps you knew the reason why

Or merely how you seemed to care.

Whilst others queued to build my load

You saw I walked a lonely road,

Rejection can taste an acid pill

That even survivors blood will spill.

So when light invades consuming dark

Flames can rise from a smallest spark!

--ooOoo

17

So there we have it in that poem, signs and signals recognised or not, and sooner or later one of the "signal makers" is going to have to make a decision or a move about or on the other person. The big problem here is that nobody likes rejection or being turned down in any way, and thus any potential move maker is very nervous about looking a fool, or even worse becoming tongue tied and sounding like a gibbering wreck!

Did I mention it could be fun? No matter for we are compelled in one way or another, with the tempting dream of eternal love and happiness, too much to resist, so the decision is made and a chance taken. A poem from my 3rd book, Reviews of Life in Verse, seems pertinent here.

Quick Decision

You are new upon my scene
I only recent for you too,
So why a special connection
Without a touch or view?

A photo can project an image
But how authentic is the shot?
And can I trust my instinct
To be the truth or not?

Yes I can get your opinions
That helps me to understand,
But I always like to rely
On the sensations of my hand.
So I would like to feel some
Vibes from perhaps a dance,
For any caress or stroking
Is more reliable than a glance.

Sensations of any nearness
With an appropriate soft touch,
Can bridge any miles in distance
Also telling you so much!

Kind words and sense of mischief
Will bring emotions into play,
And a gentle subtle teasing
Encourages folks to stay.
Especially with humour and notes
And lively words I saw,
About cheerful, emotive smiles
And an opened happy door.

But for me there is a warmth
That exudes without lies,
From a fleeting look I had
Confirmed by twinkling eyes.

--ooOoo—

The die is cast, so to speak, and two people can become a tentative couple beginning their own journey learning about each other and perhaps, more importantly, different things about themselves, and how they can feel about another person, (if this is their very first attraction stage of romance).

All exciting stuff and my last poem in this article piece, again from my 3rd book, could well be how a person comes to realise that they are in love, or like the poem title, "Stupefied"...

Stupefied

Trembling hands and pounding heart
And with every nerve end reeling,
Whenever I see or think of you
I get this strange uncertain feeling.

So drowning in your lovely eyes
Drunk and dizzy from your scent,
In a heartbeat I was taken
Not knowing what was meant,
By an apparition of such wonder
With gold clouds over you.
So I stood as before my queen
Unsure of what to say or do.

Blinking eyes and head spinning
I stood stunned beside your throne,
For I had heard of this feeling
But never thought I'd be alone.

So when my body had recovered
I thought that I should speak,
Though whatever I tried to say
Came out a senseless squeak.

Thus I had come to fully realise
All meaning of love's dream,
For while I was still shaking
I felt rooted by your beam.

So just like a nervous child
Going first time into school,
I was stunned awaiting orders
You of course looked so cool.

Then with a nod I was called over
With every sinew screaming out,
That for me the war was over
And lost to you without a doubt!

--ooOoo—

That then is my cursory introduction into the attraction part of romance and love which is one of our inherent needs as humans. Often troublesome, chaotic and on occasions painful, but never dull.

Many may try to avoid it, although overall it would be a far less interesting, and rewarding, world without its presence. For any about to embark on this journey, I offer my best wishes, and if nothing else, try to enjoy the ride!

--ooOoo--

Look Out

You can't look up as she walks by
For you know what you will see,
A probable vision of loveliness
That will attract both you and me.
But do not have guilty doubts
As most will feel just the same,
Though many try to subdue this
It is all part of life's game.

Thus recognise and enjoy attraction
Because it surely goes both ways,
And whilst can cause complications
It usually brightens up our days,
As men and women aren't meant to be
Lonely, separated, distant or apart.
Because one of the main joys in life
Is to have a happy, singing heart.

Now I do know there are doubters
As I can hear them very loud,
Deriding life's pleasures and fun
Particularly in an agreeing crowd.
But I have a very confident feeling
That if I was to place a large bet,
Most people would want romance
As without they will feel regret.

So get out in the world and smile
For it will make your face light up,
And probably be returned by others
Who may award a romantic cup,
Because they may be smiling also
In attempt to raise their attraction.
And if you can get together on this
It could give mutual satisfaction.

--ooOoo--

Call of Nature

Her touch gave him an electric shock
Down to his very heartbeat station,
And fixed a smile upon his face
Like a state of besotted inebriation.

For the feelings of love and lust
Are not so very far apart,
And while an outer sensation
It will be felt more in the heart.

So no amount of lateral thinking
Will save him from his fate,
If a pretty face and hands work,
All their magic, it's too late,
To separate rhyme or reason
So many a big man will fall,
At the first hurdle of his senses
Just as though he'd hit a wall.

For the feelings of love and lust
Are not so very far apart,
For while an outer sensation
It will be felt more in the heart.

Such is the power of natures wish
To spellbind those too ripe,
From allowing a chosen journey
Thus they must conform to type.
While surrendering any last protest
And so have to then heed the call.
For to act on their hearts wishes
Is better than not to hear at all.

--ooOoo--

Hole in the Heart

Do you have a hole in your heart
But not of a physical sort?
Although perhaps it causes pain
If you are truly left distraught,
By a reluctance to press on
With hopes and desires felt.
As recognising lost opportunities
Can cause your heart to melt.

Now it may have simply been
A venture that you missed,
Which could have been a success
Had you not gone on and kissed
Goodbye to that completion move
Of progress or financial gain.
So looking back you now believe
It was money down the drain.

Though I suspect that before this
Your heart was left with a hole,
When nerves or perhaps pride
Made you to miss an open goal,
In not asking out that somebody
Who had caught both heart and eye.
And even worse, had wanted you,
But you were too scared to try.

So now in those advancing years
You sadly remember and regret,
Not pursuing your desired lover
Which now causes great upset,
That shows in your demeanour
And moods from a soured soul.
So the whole world sees you have
A sad heart, that has a hole.

--ooOoo--

A Fabulous Fluke

A random request for information
Led to an incredible twist on a name,
That ensured blue touch paper was lit
And two lives wouldn't be the same.
For a dialogue would soon spring up
To spread like a raging forest fire,
With a sharing of respect and humour,
And more than just a touch of desire.

So for me still stunned by a connection
And rocked by wonder of a glorious find,
Your seismic attractions worked on me
To alter my soul, heart and mind,
As I had not known I looked for you
Your ways, your warmth and smiles,
With words to take my breath away
I could feel you across the miles.

And so we shared special moments
In a world that was just our very own,
When we escaped to private feelings
To have intimacies rarely known.

Now then my very special lady
You gave me many emotions new,
And I recall how my heart soared
When you said I did the same for you.

Though wonders can have bumpy roads
With periods of trials and upset,
So this may cause flames to flicker
But love we must never forget.

--ooOoo--

Sensations of Love

Not too much of an involved story behind this poem, but a nice one. For I regularly sit in my conservatory at all times of the day, and sometimes night, and often with a drink. I invariably play my "best of the Tenors" C D as I love the passion, drama and soaring voices of the music, the poet in me I guess?

When I wrote this poem I tried to capture some of that drama and "soaring Arias" in it, and also some of the passion too. Maybe you can sit quietly with a wine and enjoy the poem more now...

From lovestruck teen to an older heart
Love can arrive and catapult you,
To unscaled heights and sensations
With many vibrant feelings anew,
Soaring and gliding across the skies
Like operatic arias touching your core.
In fact you are so moved and ecstatic
You feel a need to beg for more.

So mesmerised by a dazzling light
That seems to shine right inside,
Your very secret, inner soul
Leaving nowhere left to hide.
For like a melting of frozen lakes
Washing all the icebergs away,
A controlling spirit leads you
To another rapturous day.

Thus stunned and filled with wonder
You walk majestically about,
Believing whatever comes now
Will be joyous without a doubt.
For slowly you come to realise
Some great miracle has occurred,
Brought by this faultless muse
That your whole being has stirred.

So who is this magnificent angel
And how did they spread such love?
For you now believe you're flying
Alongside passing clouds above.
The sun is now in your pocket
With many other exhilarations.
As you have come to realise
You're caught by loves sensations.

--ooOoo--

Ease of Entry

When you apply your magic touch
You take my breath away,
And take me to loves deep feelings
That don't need shades of grey.
For it's as if you have ease of entry
Into me, without need of a key.
Though that's no great mystery,
Just your unique chemistry.

So touch away sweet lady
For you have an open goal,
And an unobstructed free way
Straight into my very soul.

Though I don't think I would protest
Even if I possibly could,
Because I'm certain that no-one
Can ever be so very good
As you are, when with me,
In all our glorious connections.
For no architect of life
Could ever plan such erections,
As our love and life together
That cannot be pulled apart.
So we will travel roads together
Just living off one heart.

33

Now I know that there are doubters,
Maybe jealous of our ecstasy.
But they've probably never felt
Just what you do for me,
Or perhaps I do for you too.
If all I see in your release,
Causes such deep sensations
To give us inner peace.

--ooOoo--

The Odd Couple

She'd always wanted to be totally free
While he had always sung his song,
But strangely when vibrations met
It didn't seem unusual or wrong.
For there appeared a mutual balance
However unlikely they would ever see,
Themselves understood or believed
But such things are meant to be.

Now the lady had spent some time
Trapped in various forms of a cage,
Causing reluctance to spread her wings
Or to even turn over another page,
For experiences of stark entrapments
Can deter flying and maybe clip wings,
Although recognition of alluring vibes
Can tempt trying out new things.

Whilst the other one of this odd pair
Had cast spells and words over times,
That whilst could appear to be manifold
Only presided over soft, tender climes,
Where introductions of unknown needs
Ensured that he would re assess lives,
In much the same way Henry the Eighth
Must have appraised each of his wives?

So when two opposite and different ships
Found charted courses met up to dock,
After briefly passing in dark shadows
It seemed to cause a pleasant shock,
For when the odd couple both observed
Their companions in the separate bays,
A crossing of attractions now merged
Leading to magical future days.

--ooOoo--

Blank Pages

Do you have many blank pages
In your book of love and life?
Are they surrounded by happy lines,
Or outnumbered by times of strife?

Many people only have a slim love book,
And in fact some don't have one at all.
With no excursions into loves jungle
As they were afraid to look a fool.
But surely it's so much better
Like the saying about counting cost.
How it's worse to have never tried,
Than to have loved and lost.

So blank pages or thin volumes
Are maybe all some have to show,
For a lifetime of closed petals
So no glorious flower bloom to know,
As they kept all their inner feelings
Battened down and protected tight.
Therefore had no joyous experience
Of a loving passions might.

Thus how very sad and wasted
Is this book with its pages blank.
With nothing to say, or stories told
Only a life from which you shrank.

So no risk or dangerous adventure
Which can make heartbeats fly,
But you never quite got off the ground
As you were far too scared to try,
To let all those pent up desires
Have a freedom and make their gains,
Across skies, rivers, and mountains
Thus only a tearful book remains.

--ooOoo--

Wish

I wish that I could touch you,
Feel the texture of your skin,
Trace the contours of your body
And see where curves slope in.

I wish that I could caress you
See your reaction to a kiss,
Put in all your special places
It would be a tragedy to miss.

I wish that I could hold you
Closer if you were inclined,
To run my warm soft touches
Where a woman is defined.

--ooOoo--

Duvet

Snuggling under a duvet is a life joy
Or it can actually be bed covers too,
But however you want to use your bed
The feeling is wonderful for me and you,
Because some see it as just relaxing
Others it's purely for a good night sleep,
Though for some its a mixture of both
If they conjure up pleasures deep.

For like so many things in our lives
They're often improved or made better,
By sharing them with another person
Who may comfort or loosen the fetter,
That possible restricts or contains you
From those feelings in life you desire.
So may be achieved under the duvet,
When many nice ideas might aspire,

Thus our duvet or bedclothes covering
Can protect us from a deepest dread,
That from our childhood we have learnt
We can do by just covering our head,
And pretending we're in a defensive shell
That nothing can breach or penetrate,
As we cower safely in our sanctuary
Giving succour whatever our state.

But of course the main attraction for many
Is to share this intimate nest with another,
And without doubt the real joy of sharing
Comes to fruition with a special lover,
Who arouses and caresses your passions
That come with body to body connection,
Which has delighted both men and women,
From back in history with no correction.

Thus enjoy the duvet refuge how you will
And indulge whatever reactions it breeds,
For we are all so very different at times
So enjoy and satisfy personal needs.

--ooOoo--

HUMOUR

Social Distance Zapper

Since Coronavirus we have all been told
To social distance over two metres apart,
But that doesn't always seem to work
As some folk just won't play their part,
Which can lead us into temptation
If they crowd us, awkward like a crab.
The fat, the thin and even some small
Are then most deserving of our jab.

For if standing in a queue, or just passing
People still seem to invade your space,
Thus you need to give them a reminder
Of their distance failure and disgrace.

So when I heard about this new device
A "Social Distance Zapper" you can use,
I didn't really have much of a problem
In thinking of people I would choose,
To give out a sharp little reminder
If coming too close into my trap,
And get them to move rapidly away
When I gave them one up with my zap!

Now of course this can lead to conflict
When you play your "zapper" card,
So you may need to quickly say to them
They must stay away at least one yard,
And give you your social distance space
With a healthy area of mutual respect,
For if they fail, or agree to observe this
A zapping shock they can expect.

But naturally we must be very careful
To only use our zapper as we are taught,
For I have a fear we may end up in trouble
And on a "charge" of common assault.
Though this may all prove worthwhile
If educating the non-compliant or the bold,
So may be deserving of a zap reminder
Until they learn to do as they are told!

--ooOoo--

Left Turn Loons

We all have odd bad driving moments
But some seem totally on the moon,
And one of the very worst of these
Is the really annoying left turn loon.

Now most idiotic, or just lazy drivers
Who won't or can't bother to indicate,
Are an absolute pain in themselves
But morons not showing left complicate,
One of the simplest driving manoeuvres
That even the daftest driver can do,
Yet failure to complete this social task
Will greatly frustrate me and you.

Because as directed in the highway code
We give way to traffic coming right,
Thus we obediently sit to allow this
As non indicating cars turn out of sight.
For if they had been in any way caring
They would indicate left as they approach,
But as they turn left giving no signal
Their lack of consideration we reproach.

For as we just sit there in frustration
Having missed a safe chance to pull out,
The selfish idiot will drive carelessly on
Wondering what your wave is about.

But I guess no increased car technology
Can eradicate the berk behind the wheel,
For even if they had ability to notice
I suspect they wouldn't care or feel,
That they've been ignorant and selfish
And their driving is like a poor joke.
So our moronic cretin continues on
Without considering other folk.

--ooOoo--

Brake Light Direction

This is (another) true little background to this poem. I was struggling to find an "out of the way" place in quite a remote area, when on asking a lady she said was going right past the place, so to follow her and when got there she would put her BRAKE LIGHTS on (?), and it would be on the left.

We set off almost straight away DOWN a hill with her brake lights coming on and off, but only thick woods on my left. I decided to keep following until after a while she stopped and pointed with her HAZARD lights on! I understood her little error, but I was very grateful that she had got me there. Wonderful.

I had become confused and lost
And my Sat-Nav didn't help me,
So I stopped a lady passing by
To make my enquiring plea.
For I was surely not too far away
As I showed my intended address.
Which happily the lady knew
To keep me free from stress.

I was to follow her she said
And would indicate when there.
By putting her brake lights on,
Though at that I could only stare.

For surely you need to brake
Many times when you're driving.
So I began to get nervous again,
About if I would soon be arriving.
Especially when we had just set off
She started going down a hill,
Which brought thoughts to my mind
That this could be quite a thrill.

But strangely as she began braking
There was no turn on the left side,
Which she had told me was my cue
I was near the end of my ride.
So I just carried right on following
Her brake lights shining bright,
As I muttered a silent prayer
That this all would turn out right.

Though I need not have worried
For the lady came to a careful halt,
And gestured that my request
Was now only just a very short
Distance along where she pointed
Ant I would soon see Mantel Farm,
My destination I was driving to
And should arrive with no alarm.

So I guess this true story's moral
We'd best learn for all our sakes.
Is to trust a helpful Samaritan
Each and every time she brakes!

--ooOoo--

Space Bears

Ted and Beth are keen on space travel
And both fancy being an astronaut,
Though as ever haven't thought it through
With all you need to do, and to be taught.
But all this has never worried our Ted
Who has a confidence big as a horse,
So just assumes he can easily do it
Which we know is wrong of course.

Now Beth she isn't always so sure
But will follow her Ted to the very end,
Whatever trouble it often gets her in
Or to the difficult places it can send.

So they have both contacted NASA
And put their training applications in,
Thus are now waiting very excitably
And can't wait for their career to begin.

But sadly life doesn't always work out
And no teddy bears have been in space,
So our bears are going to be disappointed
Although for them it is no disgrace,
Because when their bad news came back
Saying that neither had been selected,
Both were sent little teddy space suits
Which they hadn't really expected.

So now they are walking about proudly
Both with helmets firmly in place,
Along with their little teddy space suits
That sadly won't be worn up in space.
But of course we've come to know
Nothing much daunts our hero bears,
Who soon forgot the disappointment
Carrying on their lives without cares.

--ooOoo--

Diddler on the Roof

I could hear a sort of banging
That was to turn out exactly right,
But nothing causing the noise
Was at that point in my sight.

It seemed to come from next door
So for my neighbour I was concerned,
But any possible noise of her banging
Had many years ago been spurned.
So did she have workmen in
Knocking her fixtures all about?
Though on checking she was safe
I confirmed that she was out.

So this racket I couldn't ignore
Clearly came from another direction,
And was really beginning to bug me
Thus called for a closer inspection,
Of all around my own property
And so I looked about outside.
To be confronted by some seagulls
Making love with a fervent pride!

Therefore it really was a banging
Causing all the noisy din,
But gulls don't know the saying
About being better out than in.
For whatever the male was doing
To make his seagull lady squeak,
It was involved and very lively
All out action with his beak.

Now I'm really not a spoilsport
And everyone shows loving proof,
Of how they feel for their partner
But why choose my roof?

So showing my authority now
And that I could also bang,
I shut my garden box loudly
With a deep resounding clang,
To stop further amorous activity
And all romantic sorties,
Hoping this would now deter
Any future sexy naughties.

For if they really must continue
They can do so without fuss,
Or I will soon be teaching them
All about coitus interrupt us.

53

For I'm really not a spoilsport
With a stuck up manner all aloof.
And I understand you need love,
But not on my chuffing roof!

--ooOoo--

Laurie Wilkinson

On or Off?

At those intimate moments in life
We have decisions that we might fear,
Such as when is the right time
To let those suitors extra near?

Maybe other little nagging worries
So you don't appear to cheat or con.
With that massive choice for men
About leaving those socks on.

Now these might seem quite simple
Little doubting thoughts and niggles.
But if arriving at inconvenient times
You won't welcome fits of giggles,
Coming loudly from your partner
That you really don't want to lose.
And you need so much to impress,
Rather than to puzzle, or amuse.

Now consideration must be given
On this great conundrum here,
So try to reduce embarrassment
And start with confidence, not fear.
But be very slow and careful
As you don't want to hear her mock.
So try to give a bit of thought
What to best do with your sock.

Now more of a decision for women
For men try their wicked way a lot.
Though how they made the lady feel
Will decide if she does or not,
Do that very precious human act
That in great emotion you can drown.
And how this plays out is simply,
If her drawers are up or down.

So back it comes to the dozy male
Trying not to make his lady scoff,
And believe me it is much preferred
To take those flipping socks OFF!

--ooOoo--

Laurie Wilkinson

Body Alive

Our living body is an amazing machine
And adapts and deals with many things,
Demanded of it during its varied life
In which time the body often sings,
Or not singing more proving its alive
That can mean quite a lot of noise.
So when in those social situations
Makes it hard to keep our poise.

Now some body noises are acceptable
Than perhaps other intimate sounds,
For nobody takes notice of a sneeze
Well before Covid 19 started its rounds.
But you get the gist of what is normal
Such as a quietly stifled little yawn,
That apart from thinking they're boring
No other embarrassment will spawn.

So even that gently controlled cough
Covered turning away, or by your hand,
Won't give concern, pre-virus of course
As mostly people will understand.

So then we look at more concerning
Noises that emulate from a live body,
Like burbling, gurgling tummy rumbles
Than can make manners seem shoddy.
For now we go a bit further into trouble
By taking a drink which you then slurp.
Or much more upsetting in company,
Is suddenly caught out by a burp.

But of course I know you're in front.
Or maybe I should perhaps say behind,
For you are well ahead of my meaning
As you attempt to help by being kind.
But I'll address the elephant in the room
Which I could not have put at the start,
Because for all men and women alike
The biggest dread is when you fart.

Yes, we all know it is quite natural
And the saying is better out than in,
But with those certain social situations
It really does seem an awful sin,
Especially If any noises go unheard
So you then think nobody could tell,
And just as you feel literally relieved
We're surrounded by a ghastly smell.

Thus now you're totally embarrassed
With your uncontrolled body noise.
But be reassured that living bodies,
Are just the same for girls and boys!

--ooOoo--

Sailor Bears

Ted and Beth now want a boat
And plan to take it out to sea,
But I know that neither can swim
So it is a very big worry to me.

They just think I'm being silly though
And said they'll be safe and sound,
But I'm not really too sure of that
As in a paddling pool nearly drowned,
So let alone going out to the open sea
With hard navigation and deep water,
Making me dread just what could happen
As they'll be like bears to a slaughter.

Naturally "Captain" Ted disputes all this
While Beth always backs him up too,
So they are still determined to go for it
And give the Coastguard more to do.

Now Ted points out all his experience
But I don't think a boat in a bath is much,
With Beth even getting panicky with that
So it's just Ted's uniformed hopes as such.
For he's no knowledge about boats at sea
But Beth still believes he can do it all.
So it seems a nautical disaster awaits
Like a sort of "ducking" before a fall.

Now I did though have one more try
To make our seafaring bears see sense,
And although they said they'd continue
I could tell they were both very tense,
With Beth clutching her water wings
That in truth she cannot quite wear.
And even Ted seemed less sure now
But determines to be a sailing bear.

So now they are all prepared to set off
With more than a little hint of doubt.
But luckily it was saved before the start,
When they saw the tide had gone out.

--ooOoo--

Beer (Article)

Beer is "probably" the most widely drunk alcoholic drink in the world, and comes only after water and tea in consumed amounts of any drink. Beer has been brewed and drunk for centuries and has always been popular for having the added advantage of being reasonably cheap and easy to produce.

There are even non-alcoholic beers now as well, and "yes" I do hear you cynics asking "why on earth do that? My guess is that it's part of our modern world of choices, political correctness and health and safety etc, but who knows?

I actually must say it does seem to me a bit like going to an orgy to play a game of cards, but each to his own...

I'm writing this article for the July publication in our "summertime" so hopefully the sun will continue to shine and initiate ideas of a nice cold beer or two, or maybe more, but I'm not counting your consumption, whether it be in a nice sunny pub garden, or perhaps your own?

Barbecues, social gatherings, at "the pub", drowning sorrows, Dutch courage, flirtations, celebrations and countless other occasions are where beer is drunk, or maybe even used in several of the above, (you choose ho ho) situations. Whatever the circumstance, I think beer is deeply embedded in our culture and the lives of most people today. Do you agree?

First poem then and it just has to be "Have Another Beer" from my 3rd book Reviews of Life in Verse...

Have Another Beer

The weather is not great
And through the rain we peer,
It is getting us all down
So have another beer.

We want to drive away
But roads are blocked I hear,
There are far too many cars
So let's have another beer.

A trip up to the shops
To join the thronging crowd,
And mad folks with their trolleys
Make you want to curse aloud!
So you stay at home to book
A holiday, not too dear,
But the internet is down
Best to have another beer.

Then you're on the phone
Many options now to choose,
It's enough to drive you mad
And go back on the booze.
They say you're in a queue
But your turn is nowhere near,
I can't be doing this
So I'll have another beer.

Thus there's so many things
In life to drive you mad,
So have another beer then
You just won't feel so bad!

--ooOoo--

Thus have another beer then, perhaps the answer for some in genuine sentiments with maybe no "upper limit" or time to stop, but of course not for us "veritable paragons" of behaviour I suspect?

Talking of "behaviours", I suppose I have to look at "lager louts" on drinking sprees that are seemingly causing mounting problems in our town centres at night, and some of the television programmes showing these antics are not much short of horrifying and almost unbelievable. Sadly they are a true fact and we surely soon must have some more tougher measures of control, but once again I assume it's the way "things are going" and will run its course? Mmmmmmm ?

Anyway moving on a bit from that and coming back to beer, which obviously is behind a lot of inappropriate drinking bouts, there now appears to be a trend to just get as drunk as possible as soon as possible with the use of "shots" and strong drinks being consumed very quickly to do so, instead of a more deliberate pace of beer drinking. So here's an insight of just what can happen is in my poem "Booze and Two's" from my 3rd book entitled Reviews of Life in Verse...

Booze and Two's

It is written that alcohol increases desire
But reduces performance too,
This can be proved on most weekends
When the drunkards roll into view.

Inhibitions and balance both fade
The harder they drink and revel,
With love in the air and emotions high
And skirts raised to panties level,
On young ladies mostly so serene
And always shy of the sexy scrum.
But with lots of drink inside them now
They're more than keen to flash their bum!

Blokes also will feel the effect
As more alcohol lowers their wit.
Thinking they're great lovers and Romeo's
But in truth most are not even fit.
Though that doesn't stop them at all
Trying to show off all their might,
With them struggling to just stand up
Let alone trying to fight.

Yes alcohol can always take its toll
Making a fool out of me and you,
For I've never been to bed with an ugly girl
But woken up with quite a few.

--ooOoo—

A bit of a "tongue in cheek" joke there with that *old chestnut* before they come to "take me away", but heaven forbid we are ever totally prevented from having a sense of humour.

Yes "good old alcohol" then but it can and should be just a sociable relaxing pleasure, but we all make our choices in life, and even with that we can choose how we drink our beer, with personalised or preferred receptacle of, pot, glass, straight or with a handle or pewter pot etc etc.

Anyway, another poem before I close this from my latest book Poet Reveals All...

Love and Alcohol

When love comes crashing in your life
It can take you over as a whole.
But if disappearing much too fast,
You may be left with just alcohol.

For love has a way of changing life
And all the things that you do,
Though of course will introduce
Many things done with two.

So if you had been quite content
With life that was safe and sure,
It might be sadly hard to return
To where you were before.
And all those solid friends you had
May have drifted, or felt driven away.
As they didn't seem to fit any more
With your love life day to day.

So when bewildered from the shock
Of your love now disappeared.
You may stroll about inconsolably,
Feeling everything seems weird.

Thus you might seek some solace
In a glass for quite a while,
As you desperately try to adjust
Whilst longing for a smile,
From anyone who seems to care
And has sympathy for your tears.
Because the fact is you're now alone,
With only alcohol to say "cheers"!

--ooOoo—

So that is that then on beer, so Cheers before "Time Gentlemen Please", and "No more orders at the bar"...

--ooOoo—

Bell End

I loved my football from an early age
And began to regularly go to matches,
Though being small and young in years
Often watched the games in snatches.
For in big crowds it was hard to see
Though you might be let down the front,
So I mostly got a good view
Amongst the crowds push and shunt.

Now I don't recall actually when
That I decided to get a bell,
Which I bought down the market
And it would raise devils in their hell.
Some people would have a rattle
Which made a clanking sound,
But I'm sure that Laurie's bell
Was heard all across the ground.

So I felt quite chuffed with this
Though I had begun to realise,
It wasn't popular with everyone
Because of its ring, and not the size,
Which wasn't that particularly big
But the clang was really loud.
Again not pleasing all about me,
Though I felt very proud.

The trouble, and the bells demise
Came about when we scored a goal,
In a very close, important game
So I rang out heart and soul.
But tragically I went too mad
And hit a big bloke in the face,
Who wasn't pleased and threatened
To put my bell up a personal place.

Thus that really spelt the sad end
Of me taking my bell with me,
As the crowd were mostly regulars
So the same people I would see.

Which invoked prudence over courage
Although I did think about a drum,
But I worried if I got one of those
The bloke might shove it up my bum.
So I decided to just shout out loud
Like others, who would also sing.
And though I still enjoyed myself
I really missed my bell to ring!

--ooOoo--

Beth's Green Eye

Now Ted and Beth are a happy couple
Sharing adventures and are lovers too,
Which really suits their teddy lives
Supporting each other in all they do.

But lately Beth has had some doubts
About just how her teddy boy feels,
Because she thinks he's gone a bit distant
Not always joining her for their meals,
And at times also seems a bit distracted
Looking thoughtfully out into space,
Which has got our Beth quite worried
As they always share a special place.

Worse than this in Beth's uncertain mind
In that Ted is talking to Sleepy Bear a lot,
So she's getting a bit envious and unhappy
About any subversive romantic plot,
That appears to involve Sleepy Bear
Who she always gets on with very well,
But is now worried she may be a rival
Although for certain she can't tell.

But we can know what lovely Beth can't
Well for a little while at the very least,
As her true love is arranging a big event
For her, because his love hasn't ceased,
And so as it's her birthday very soon
Ted is organising a massive surprise,
Which is why he chatted to Beth's friend
To help delight the apple of his eyes.

So finally the big day came around
When Beth had lived for another year,
And was ecstatic, overjoyed and excited
That her friends came from far and near.
Which was all down to her lovely Ted
Contacting all of their bear friends,
To come and see Beth on her birthday
And share their love that never ends.

Of course Beth did feel a tiny bit guilty
About getting herself in a jealous tether,
When she should have known all along
She and Ted will be happy for ever.

--ooOoo--

Ode to Sylvie's Ears

A radio presenter role is not all joy
In fact it can be laced with fears,
With also discomfort in the heat
And headphones causing sweaty ears.
Now obviously that's not too pleasant
As we all know that sweat leaks,
But Sylvie carries on professionally
Hiding all traumas as she speaks.

Of course there are other difficulties
Which may interrupt your goals,
Like having a crazy poet on air
To start you talking about toilet rolls.
But again you cheered the airways
With your pleasant humour and style,
That allows you personal pleasure too
Playing country music for a while.

But sweaty ears and crazy poets
Don't happen every day or week,
So listen to Sylvie on Radio Sussex
But that tuning dial don't tweak.
For she will see if you have gone
Or who is listening to her show.
Ensuring it's all a fun filled time,
With sweaty ear bits we won't know

--ooOoo--

No Hiding Place

The story behind this poem is very amusing I think, and the poem from it is always well received at my "Reading Gigs".

After a European decision that large swimming trunks (boxer shorts style) for men were unhygienic in pools (as men were apparently getting straight in the water with work shorts on), it was decreed that men must wear "Speedo" style, or brief swimming trunks in swimming pools, thus many had to squeeze into "too often too small" brief trunks.

This poem is my take on it...

At our local swimming pool
You can see many a curious sight.
With lots of lovely young girls,
Whilst other scenes are a fright.

Men wearing tight fitting trunks,
"Budgie Smugglers" for the thin.
Though sadly worn by some "largies"
Having more hanging out, than in!
For it seems a life contradiction
That the larger many folk grow,
Instead of tucking it safely away
They must put it all out on show.

Now I'm not against big sizes
I have a growing waist myself,
But I fervently try to hide it
Not put it on the front shelf.

But back to those swimming trunks
Of varying size of modesty cover,
And the battle of those bulges
Where some really need another
Or much larger piece of cloth,
To keep their harvest all intact.
For hiding mountains behind a stamp
Won't work, and that's a fact!

--ooOoo--

Chariot Wheels

Shopping trolleys are inanimate
I want to make that clear,
They really cannot be blamed
If pushed by a Boadicea

Waddling largies push these carts
Like Rommel with his tanks,
And should you be in line of attack
You must dodge with little thanks.

Whether you are in or out the store
The dangers just the same,
Except inside there is little room
And much less chance to complain.

Outside in the widespread terrain
Your worry is their speed,
Or the lack of route or direction
So look out or you will bleed!

Propelled with gusto by the hulks
They roar across the road,
And doesn't need a genius to see
They don't know the Highway Code.

The shopping trolley chariot race
Should fill your heart with fear,
For driven by these Amazon's
Even Ben Hur would not go near!

So stepping back inside the shop
You should feel no need to beg,
Until an unseeing Genghis Khan
Shoves their trolley in your leg.

Little old ladies are just as bad
And be sure you are no freer,
For they've no idea where to push,
And you they can't see or hear.

These rattling supermarket trains
That is the shoppers trolley,
In themselves are little threat
Only when trundled by a wally,
Of whom there seems to be a horde
Not knowing where there going,
And don't see or care for us
Who risk all by our unknowing.

That to survive the trolley dash
You must forget all manners,
And do your very best to avoid
Trolley chariots and their banners!

--ooOoo--

Ted and Beth's Fishing Trip

Ted decided that he would go fishing
As his plan to sail a boat had failed,
Because he and Beth had got worried
And as the tide was out hadn't sailed.

So now Ted is taking a reluctant Beth
To go and hopefully catch some fish,
But Beth isn't too enthralled with the idea
As it's not exactly what she would wish,
Spending time on a cold, wet river bank
While an enthusiastic Ted casts out his line.
For as usual he is all confident and sure,
But Beth's mood is not too sublime.

Especially when Ted gives an angry shout
As he gets his line caught up in a tree,
Because although he brags and swaggers
It so often goes very wrong you'll see,
For now he can't free his tangled line
However hard he pulls at it and tugs.
So he is angrily forced to give it up
Muttering teddy words as he shrugs.

So Beth says its best that they go home
But Ted won't hear of any such wish,
Saying he has got many other fishing lines
And will not go until catching some fish,
So the determined, cross look on his face
Fills our Beth with frustration and worry,
As she knows he might now stay all night
If he doesn't get a fish catching flurry.

Now unusually for them they start to argue
And Beth's patience is getting much shorter,
Until with an anguished and startled shout
Ted slips and falls into the muddy water,
Initially sending Beth into laughing hysterics
Seeing him soaking wet, with an angry frown,
But then her laughter turns into worried fear
As she panics her Ted could drown!

But Beth's helping paw aids Ted to get out
Although a much sadder and wiser bear,
Who is learning another painful lesson
About cockiness and him taking more care.
So unhappily our bears traipse off home
With Ted still in quite a little teddy strop,
But Beth knows just how to cheer him up
And buys fish and chips from a shop!

--ooOoo--

Laurie Wilkinson

Sofa so Good

There are times to change your sofa
And splash out on that new settee,
So I am writing about it now
As it has just been done by me.

But it really isn't that simple
For they must be changed over too,
Getting rid of the old one first
Which can be a battle before you do,
Because what seemingly came in easy
May not go out quite the same,
As you have added shelves and carpets
But your old sofa can't remain.

For you have the new one coming
Which means you need the space,
Being taken up by the old one
So it is now a desperate race,
Though with just a little thought
And some extra care now spent,
You can get the old one removed
Thus no expletives are vent.

So with worthy paid for muscle
The exchange is successfully done,
Which means you use your new one
And that kicks off some more fun.
For where your "botty" happily sat
Over many a week and long year,
You must now wriggle and move
Towards perfect comfort cheer.

But finally it all goes very well
Just like a settee exchange should,
So you sit content and contemplate
That it's all sofa so good!

--ooOoo--

Laurie Wilkinson

REFLECTION

The Parrot and the Poser

A parrot is a natural, multi-coloured bird
That has increasingly become a popular pet,
Because of their vibrant and florid look
And amount of verbal mimicking you get,
If you give them your time and attention
Talking to your parrot to help become tame.
For they are mostly an accommodating bird
Always up for some fun and a game.

They can also be encouraged to leave the cage
And fly around the room and return again,
Possibly even landing on your hand to eat
Should you make a determined effort to train,
This beautiful bird originally from the tropics
Who seem to soon domestically settle down,
And become great company for the owners
To ensure that they'll smile and not frown.

Now there is a comparable sort of person
Whose habits can mirror the parrot's mould,
For this is certainly and extrovert person
Called posers because they're loud and bold,
Attracting all attention they possibly can,
To almost say just look and listen to me.
But many people will try extremely hard
To avoid them and attempt to flee.

For nobody likes bragging show-offs
Always boasting about all that they do,
But this is often only their imagination
For very little of it turns out to be true.
Although this never daunts our poser
Strutting about with a petty little act,
Which has folk yawning, or even worse
Turning away bored, and that's a fact.

So on one hand we have a pretty parrot
A joy to behold in colours so bright,
But on the other a poser driving us insane
With his annoyingly daft attention fight,.
For most people love the natural way
Especially if like a parrot's florid grace,
Unlike a pretentious poser of the world
That people avoid having to face.

--ooOoo--

Fish on a Bike

Some images are just too implausible
Yet we often use them to give a view,
Of a ridiculous descriptive point
That any sane mind won't pursue.

Like the saying of a fish on a bike
Or the proverbial bag of snakes,
Which we all know is a bit bizarre
But as counter argument often makes,
Reinforced improbability of someone
Doing the job just as you would like.
So the chance of that ever happening,
Is as likely as a fish riding a bike.

Thus we use many florid descriptions
Mostly in a reverse psychology way,
Like people "useful as a chocolate teapot",
And such sayings will brighten our day.
For a heavy downpour or rainstorm
Is described as raining cats and dogs,
And just who can forget an odd person
Said to be as mad as a box of frogs?

There are lots of other sayings as well
Adding more colour to what we say,
Like in taking advantage of opportunity
And when the sun shines make our hay,
Which is probably quite an old suggestion
Going right back to our language roots,
Such as when things are all going well
We're advised to go fill our boots.

Getting "into the swing" with this now
I could possibly cover more ground,
Which brings another saying to mind
And that is as "sound as a pound".
For saying people are daft as a brush
Or blind as a bat, can add to the log,
And may lead to someone who is ill
Being described as sick as a dog.
Thus it seems the list is quite endless
Almost as far as the eye can see.
But I don't want to make a mistake,
And go barking up the wrong tree.

So best I end this ode of sayings now
Or else go on like "Tennyson's Brook",
Though I'm quite sure it will amuse you
And be noted as worth a second look.
For you might keep your eyes peeled
Or be dry as a bone, is another I like.
But I must admit my favourite saying,
Is that of the fish riding a bike.

--ooOoo--

For Fathers

A father is so much more than a name
For there can be a very special bond,
Between a daughter or a son
Who can grow up especially fond
Of this figure who guides them along
Those early years, and even for life,
In his attempts to love and protect
Whilst keeping them free from strife.

Because any man can become a father
It's just a simple biological fact,
But to become a proper father and dad
There has to be a very committed pact
Of love, care and a deep devotion
Which may not always seem returned.
Although constant unconditional love
Can ensure magic rewards are earned.

Now I was fortunate to have a father
Both dedicated and also a great friend.
And thus appreciated all of our times,
So precious, and almost without end
Around my happy and witty role model
Teaching lessons I would never forget,
Because this special relationship shared,
We would never cheat on, or regret.

Now I'm quite sure I've passed that on
To the treasured gift of my son,
Who didn't always seem to comply
Even at times targeting me for fun,
In his jokes and childish pranks
But as he matured he cast that aside.
So my heart swells when he now says
That he looks on me with pride.

Thus please indulge your dear old dad
Who will do so much for you,
For it can be a lonely world without him
And that's a sad fact, but very true.
So whether it is those special times
Or maybe an incredible hobby taught,
Ensure you enjoy those precious moments
For a father's love just can't be bought.

--ooOoo--

Open Up

This quite a happy little story of when I was staying at my fixed caravan on a site in France, (it amuses me that they're called "Mobile Homes" but aren't mobile, unless on a lorry), some time ago, about 2014 as poem is in my second book More Poetic Views of Life.

Anyway the weather had been awful, raining non-stop for a few days so I felt I just had to go out on my bike during a slight lull. True to form after about 30 minutes it absolutely poured down again, and anticipating this I took refuge in a bar.

Using my very best "pigeon French" I ordered a beer only to be told the owner and two Belgium customers spoke excellent English and we all had a great chat and a few beers. Riding back, again in pouring rain I composed this poem in my head until I got back.

I'm so glad that I spoke to you
How else would I have known,
Thoughts that you have told me
Which are all your very own?

You shared just what you think
What makes you laugh or cry,
Some things that make you angry,
That you love, or perhaps let by.

Now we can often pass each other
Without a smile or spoken word,
And that we don't talk to each other
Is quite frankly so absurd.

We need to share our feelings
And how others may endure.
For in a world of madness
It's good to know what's pure.
By listening and talking
We learn some different views,
Like how life can be for others
When before we had no clues.

Now we can often pass each other
Without a smile or spoken word,
And that we don't talk to each other
Is quite frankly so absurd.

So give a nod, or even smile
Who knows what may pan out?
You may have great times spent
If you end your speaking drought!

--ooOoo--

One Voice

I woke to the disappointment
Of rain hammering my mobile home,
For a storm seemed right overhead
And was pounding the roof dome.
So I turned over and back to sleep
To awake again in another hour,
But sadly the rain had not ceased
And thus my mood was sour.

But laying in bed hearing the din
A minor miracle then occurred,
For against the noise on my roof
Came the sweet singing of a bird.
A solitary chirping of morning joy
From a little chap I couldn't see,
But the song he continually sang
Was a great delight to me.

Though what had motivated this bird
Whose song beat the noisy rain,
I'm sure I will never really know
But he kept up with his refrain.
Now I'm no great bird expert
So couldn't tell the type or family,
But because he sang out in a storm
His form I didn't need to see.

For soon a couple of other birds
Joined in with the singular voice,
Maybe encouraged and led by him
Or perhaps just their own choice.

So now against a strong backdrop
Of rain clattering on my roof,
I had this wonderful little choir
Singing out in beautiful proof,
That even in our dismal times
A determined song by one voice,
Can overcome depressive scenes
To offer a happier choice.

--ooOoo--

You Can't Wear Your Hat In Here

I grew up in a time of more formal etiquette
Like always taking your hat off indoors,
And men walked on the outside of women
But these were social guidelines not laws.

Now times have obviously moved on
So behaviours and manners are now changed,
And this all largely occurs with no problems
With ideas and fashions also re-arranged.
For example men now do wear hats inside
As I did recently when going in for a beer,
But to my utter shock and surprise was told
That you can't wear that cap in here!

A security guard was giving the order
For sadly many venues have these in place,
Which gives some indication of current times
To probably mark out a prevailing disgrace,
Of over-inebriated lack of respectful control
When out and about in villages and towns,
That I think personally particularly sad
As I much prefer smiles to frowns.

But back to my error of wearing a cap
As I stepped inside that hostelry bar,
To be so abruptly challenged on my attire
Which I had worn happily near and far.
Though now it seems this is not allowed
And confused me to a level of disbelief,
When it was explained that the main reason
Is that hats may have weapons underneath.

Now I think that I'm generally quite aware
Although I don't stay out so late at nights,
On most evenings, or only the occasional time
Which seems just as well now as some sights
Are apparently not pleasant and quite dangerous,
With increased drunkenness, brawls and affray.
For though not always peaceful where I grew up
It was never near out of control like today.

So I did get an inkling of life concerns now
To make me aware of behaviours and fear,
And not to put any weapon under my cap
For you can't wear your hat in here.

--ooOoo--

A Knock Upon My Door

I got an unexpected knock on my door
But not literally at my actual dwelling.
For although not directly at my address,
It was mine, with new situations spelling
Loudly out for me, but not clearly at first,
And with no clues to what would be sent.
But there could be no misunderstanding
That the knock was for only me meant.

So it would seem I would be on a journey
Although in reality I wouldn't go very far
In actual distance or any new horizons,
But on a life trial that would leave a scar,
From situations and emotions new to me
As I had to be a rock and totally devoted,
To my freshly ordained life commitment
Of which I was unaware and hadn't voted.

For life will rarely give too much warning
About any little sly suggestions or clues,
So off I went on my new designated role
And completely changed life I didn't choose.
But still that wasn't able to protect me
Or fend off all of my tribulations anew,
That came in an increasing bombardment,
So I was left not knowing what to do.

100

But true to say, and in my defence
I devoutly tried to do my very best,
Battling on many challenging fronts
With very little relief, or much rest.

Because if the unfortunate side of life
Comes to visit you, no matter what for,
Please then have some sympathy for me
And that unexpected knock upon my door.

--ooOoo--

Sleep (article)

Sleep, or lack of it affects us all, probably dictating many of our moods, concerns and perhaps even our behaviour and actions. Some of this may be down to the fact that it is etched on our psyche for the paramount need to have a really good night's sleep. I'm not sure it's as simple as that and clearly, like many things in life, what is a really good sleep for one person may not be the case for others.

Of course we all feel better after a sound and restful sleep, but, are we going to suffer that much without it? Not long periods without sleep obviously, (and the well documented use of "sleep deprivation" for hostages and prisoners highlights this), but the ordinary and everyday person, if they actually exist. Well, whether they do or not it doesn't matter, for again I believe the answer comes down to individuals and their varying ability to sleep, and perhaps more importantly, their concept of it!

I suspect, like most people I have friends and acquaintances with a variety of sleep contentment, or lack of it, (see it IS very much discussed), with some sleeping for quite a few hours, others much less. Obviously if there is a pattern of unsatisfactory or disturbed sleep it can have adverse reactions. Before we consider that, I think we should look at the whole picture and not worry or panic as some people seem to, which naturally exacerbates the situation.

Time for my first poem and aptly called "Awake" from my 6th book, Poet Reveals All...

Awake

Oh why am I fully awake?
When the world around me sleeps,
So what is going on in my head
That from my slumber keeps?

I was tired when I went to bed
With my eyes trying to close.
But I still awoke very early
Which started off my woes.
Because I just couldn't return
To that lovely land of sleep,
With many thoughts disturbing me
And from any peace did keep.

So at first I just lay there quietly
As my mum had said, was resting.
But the failure to drop off again
My agitated mood was testing.

For I was now needing to resort
To my tried and tested ploys,
Like a hot milky drink, and music
And a return to sleeping joys.
But sadly all attempts failed
As I couldn't get back off again,
Which started to cause concern
In case I went insane.

Thus another tactic was needed
In attempt not to shout and curse.
For I just started to write again,
And produced this piece of verse!

--ooOoo—

So that's about staying awake should you stir from your slumbers, but I guess many people would settle for that as they complain of not even getting to sleep in the first place.

Other complaints I've read or heard of consist of very light sleep that is easily disturbed, or people who wake very early, (often a feature of depression), even if they don't get to sleep until late, or with fractured sleep patterns, short term sleep or in extreme cases, no sleep at all.

These problems can involve all ages apparently, although it is a generalisation that you need more sleep in younger than older years. A much bigger problem, if it is allowed to become a major issue, is to let it become an obsession, but of course that depends on any resulting knock on effects!

Another poem then and this is from my 4th book "Life Scene in Verse" with the poem called "Sleep Perchance".

Sleep Perchance?

We all love and need our sleep
Perchance to dream as the bard said,
So just relax and prepare to rest
When you put yourself to bed.

For sleep they say, is a great healer
And recharges both body and mind,
To feel refreshed in a healthy way
Maybe to solve problems too, I find.
For we're also advised in life
To "sleep on" a decision I hear,
But whether this is true or not
In the morning things seem clear.

Thus allow yourself to drift away
And to slip into a world of dreams,
Maybe to caress those hidden thoughts
So all will not be as it seems.
Then allow the visions of your deep
To take you soaring to the moon,
In a fluttering of warm sensations
You awaken from much too soon.

So just relax and prepare to escape
When laying down to sleep,
For if you can lose yourself in peace
Great councils you will keep.

--ooOoo--

That is all well and good, but if you do have a sleep problem it will invariably get worse the more it's worried about and, whilst easier to say than do, it is recognised as being very true. My mum had an answer, as many wonderful mothers do with problems, and used to say to me not to worry too much if I couldn't sleep, but just lay there as at least you are resting, and if you don't sleep well tonight, you will probably catch it up tomorrow.

I am sure her advice was correct for me because apart from odd occasions when I had a serious worry, I have always, and continue to now have, an excellent sleep pattern.

Maybe this next poem from my 3rd book, Reviews of Life in Verse, is a bit too abstract if you cannot sleep, but with tongue firmly in my cheek, I repeat that I have an excellent sleep pattern. I've given some clues, suggestions and advice a little further on in this article, so if you need it or are still awake, read on to "Beam of Love".

Beam of Love

In the darkness now I think of you
Though you may be near or far.
And if I saw you would I know,
If you're my missing star?

For it is very hard to find someone
If you don't know how they look.
For I have never seen or met you,
Or found a description in a book.

So maybe that's why in the dark
I fantasise I feel your breath,
Because I'm denied sight or sound
Thus think you're a gift from death.

Though you are not here to touch
And however hard I try to see,
I know you, my mysterious spirit,
Are watching and waiting for me.

In the darkness now I think of you
Though you may be near or far.
So if I saw you how would I know,
If you're my missing star?

Why do I feel your shadowy form
As if you are all around my bed?
So where have you come from,
To be inside my head?

Thus I'm making a request to meet
Whatever time, or in a dream.
Perhaps you'll come and take me
To love by the moons night beam.

For now I know what the truth is,
You're a figment of imagined love,
Someone I met, though didn't see
Who'll be there in the stars above!

--ooOoo--

Perhaps that is not for you, but I enjoyed it and I sleep the good sleep nearly every night, so over to you then!

I will though keep my promise from earlier and repeat some advice on getting a good night's kip, and these include; good exercise during the day, a milky drink before bed, trying to keep a clear conscience or more rationally putting things into context, (when awake in the night the problems will seem much larger). Try to deal with, or at least have a practicable plan for resolving, any ongoing concerns and worries. Again, easier said than done, but if a problem exists it has to be dealt with.

For my part, possibly with my "30 years working in psychiatry" hat on, I believe that if you have a "happy heart and head" you will generally have; quite good health, sleep well and be all round a content and settled little "bunny" or person...

Last poem coming up, and if you cannot sleep, then this poetic "advice" maybe ideal for you? Yes alright, I have now removed my tongue totally from my cheek, but will continue to smile as I mostly do.

All Through the Night

Sometimes only just to kiss you
Won't make you feel alright.
So I have to state my intention,
To hold you through the night.

Which I hope will delight you
As much as it does for me.
So we must wait for morning
When we can then clearly see,
If our ensuing love was great
For both of us to have gains,
As it's now my main ambition
To ensure our love remains.

So don't be shocked at my ardour
As it is meant for me to show,
How much I want to love you
And not let our ecstasy go.
Because sometimes love is taken
For granted, causing disgrace.
But you can see I'm determined
That ours will stay in place.

But you need now to do nothing
More than you think is right,
When I tell you once again
I will hold you through the night.
Which I hope will reassure you
How my love is always bold.
So just lay back and enjoy it,
Along with my night long hold.

--ooOoo—

Here ends "my epistle" on sleep, and knowing you all to be veritable "pillars of society" I'm sure that you all sleep well and like the proverbial baby.

If not, goodnight and I will think and dream of you! I'm that sort of poet.

Goodnight then, ZZZZZzzzzzzzzzzzzzzzzzzzz.

--ooOoo--

Questioning Fate

I really don't know why I'm here
Although my parents love did devote,
But nobody had asked my opinion
And so I never got to have a vote.
Thus here I am on my life journey
Which I admit has been mostly good,
Though at times I do question it all
If things are not easily understood.

So we arrive in this diverse world
And must set out along our way,
With feelings of great bemusement
At the new things to learn each day.
For nothing seems to stay the same
As technology changes all we know,
To make us despair in utter frustration
And we're tempted to just let go.

Hopefully other places are more settled
And not always difficult and confusing,
For whenever we seem to catch It all up
Changes ensure that we keep losing.
So we must now do our very best
Not to get all left out, or fall behind,
Though just as we solve one problem
Other conundrums cloud our mind.

Also we see our family and friends die
Or get cut down with some cruel disease,
That robs them of mobility or senses
With cancer and dementia leaders of these
Despicable inflictions that lurk in wait,
To cause us distress and sometimes fear,
As we get older and must struggle along
To wonder again, just why are we here?

--ooOoo--

Snakes and Ladders

A bit like a snakes and ladders game
With direction arrows across the floor,
To show you the designated direction
So best you don't try to find the door,
Because that only has the one way out
Something similar to a confusing maze.
Where you wander round in confusion
And so will only end up in a daze.

For this is the world prevailing now
As we take precautions against Covid 19,
This new silent but very deadly killer
And something the world has never seen,
Because it passes from person to person
Ensuring that we all must stay apart,
As in a massive leper's colony now
Causing absence to break any heart.

So along with many other direct orders
To keep our distance and to wear a mask,
Supermarkets also had a one way system.
That soon turned out to be quite a task,
Keeping to your own side or direction,
Especially when others don't seem to care,
For at times we just look on in frustration
At people ahead who shouldn't be there.

And so on and on continued the charade
With people compliant or just ambivalent,
In trying to follow the indicated route
Getting harder to see what it all meant,
In a confusion having questionable value
Whilst causing people to become quite irate,
At the floor game of noughts and crosses
Making us feel we were all in checkmate!

--ooOoo--

Not To Reason Why

Loyal boots march where they're told
On rough terrain or forbidding ground,
For our courageous forces go
To where danger's often found.

Never to disobey or question
Any strange command given out,
No matter how they feel
Or how much that they doubt,
The wisdom of the orders
And so their best they'll try,
To perform for Queen and country
For they will just do or die.

Now these heroes all have families
Who miss them when away,
From loving parents worrying
To wives who save the day,
By keeping safe their houses
Also looking after any kids,
With school runs and homework
And preventing escaping bids.

So all of this is on the mind
Of our service personnel,
Who thinking of all those at home
Must face all kinds of hell.
From heat and dust with full kit on
To those unseen exploding mines,
Or seemingly friendly children
Who with the enemy combines.

Loyal boots march where they're told
On rough terrain or forbidding ground,
For our courageous forces go
To where danger's often found.

Now what is it we may ask
That brings so much commitment here?
With comradeship and loyalty
To those who share their beer.
But it is something more than this
Maybe not understood by me and you,
When these mixed background heroes
Decide there's a job to do.

--ooOoo--

Figment

I have a vivid imagination now
And can believe many things are true,
For if you obsess on them enough
They may become reality for you.

So I guess they could be called dreams
These figments tantalising my mind,
As I have had such thoughts before
But they were all of a different kind,
For now my dreams and figments
Seem to be separating into two,
With one type I can awake from
But the other I'm convinced is true.

Thus please excuse and allow me
My starstruck and bewildered gaze,
For I am mostly now completely lost
Attempting to find exits to this maze,
Of controlling thoughts and ideas
Sprouting up to stimulate my soul.
But at times they mock and laugh
At my delusion of such a goal.

Now please don't get the papers ready
As I can assure you I am not mad,
But yes, that is what they all say
In various experiences I have had.
So maybe some rubbed off on me
Or did I learn how to play the game?
But whichever way I consider it,
The answer is exactly the same.

So please again allow my explanation
Of how my mind and imagination work,
Because although at times it bothers me
They really ensure that I cannot shirk,
My ability, or perhaps now a mission
Writing to help explain life for others.
As it also gives me tremendous pleasure,
If giving comfort like their mothers.

--ooOoo--

Brash Banned

This poem centres on my thoughts of a quite odious person I met, as described in the poem, but was also abundantly rude and declared would "say what they liked" to other people but certainly didn't like it if the same was done to them.

Unfortunately after they were rude to me I reciprocated in the very same manner, (quite unusual for me these days), said my eloquent piece, and no it didn't go down very well, but never mind eh?

The small minded person says a lot
And whilst smiling must be brash,
Shouting out they speak their mind
But if challenged they'll soon crash.
For to give out insults and be smart
You have to be strong like a stack.
And also prepared to accept grief,
If others words come straight back.

I was always taught to share a joke
And bandy humour off like a spout.
But the massive lesson of this game,
Is to take what you have given out.

Sadly some people don't get this fact
And bellow out just what they feel.
But should you dare to criticise them
They soon moan and start to appeal.
For mostly these crass people brag
In a hypocritical way of getting by.
And believe they've the right to abuse,
But on the receiving end they'll cry.

I was always taught to share a joke
And bandy humour off like a spout.
But the massive lesson of this game
Is to take what you have given out.

So we can see their spiteful words
They aim cowardly at all other folk.
Never to see the humour or irony,
That upset they'll whinge and choke.

--ooOoo--

Born Anew

I'm confronted by crossroads and junctions
When I would prefer one straight lane,
Because these various direction choices
Are not helping me much to stay sane.

For many ideas and choices avail me
Since I have left the clinging mire.
Leaving me in quite a bewilderment
As to what is now my heart's desire.

Because I had spent so long battling
To be both caring and master of all,
And that is an almost impossible task
From which it so very easy to fall,
Into bouts of exhaustion and frustration
That watching eyes may fail to see,
Yet doesn't always stop any observers
From criticism, but not helping me.

For though support services are about
And apparently can do everything,
But it doesn't always actually occur
However often their bell you ring.
Though to be fair that isn't entirely true
For a few people really did care,
But whilst they did grease the wheels
Much needed help just wasn't there.

So therefore I now look out anew
A sadder, tired, but wiser man,
Confronted by changes in a new world
Like some sort of older "Peter Pan".

And so not to be daunted or afraid
I step out to see if I will win or lose,
But all seems muddled and confusing,
Like the road that I must choose.

--ooOoo--

Beam

There is a beam of light I follow
Allowing me to cast doubt asunder,
For it makes me believe in miracles
As I walk in majesty and wonder.
So all the ills that prey on the world
Can't touch me in my ecstatic joy,
Donated by my magic light beam
That makes me a happy boy.

Because when people don't believe me
I am still guided by this bright beam,
Which can take me over completely
So things aren't as bad as they seem,
And that in itself is a small miracle,
Most people would probably desire,
Instead of wading through a darkness
Or up to their necks in a mire.

So now I have a bigger conundrum
For if my sort of light sabre is real,
How do I go about explaining it
As I'm regularly asked how I feel?
Well I'm fairly settled, still standing
Though my world became quite hard,
Which all considered puzzles me too
How I still have a happy ace card.

Laurie Wilkinson

Thus back I go to the drawing board
With the perpetual questions on there.
For again I cannot answer them at all,
But with my light beam I don't care!

--ooOoo--

Ladders

A ladder helps you up in the world
But that is mostly only in height,
Though there is also a step ladder
Which gets you up with less fright,

Though of course just like in life
Ladders may get you right up there,
But also bring you down again
With a jolt if not taking any care.
So the simple ladder should remain
As a largely simple purpose aid,
To get you up high or on a roof
With safety precautions made.

Because with ladders and heights
There are always risks to be taken,
So we must check to minimise these
If not to fall and end up badly shaken,
Or worse as can quite easily happen
If the ladder isn't placed safe and sure.
Also the climber needs to concentrate
So as to not end up on the floor.

Now this all sounds very simple
And to be quite honest so it should,
For if all precautions are taken
The ladder's use will be all good.

Though there is another consideration
With a comparison of ladders to man,
As sometime even with a simple job
Humans will get it wrong if they can.
With also that true old adage told
Many times and with great renown,
That best to remember what goes up
Can quite easily come back down.

For this could possibly be a lesson
To people who think they know it all,
As life can often bring us back down
With pride going before a fall.

--ooOoo--

TRAGEDY

Armistice

I would like a break or an armistice
Even a respite, but please don't scoff,
For I feel a bit like that old sixties film
Called "stop the world I want to get off".
Because sometimes you feel swept along
A bit like flotsam on a rushing tide,
Leaving you helpless and out of control
With an uneasy feeling inside.

For on the occasions life is hectic
And all seems manically gushing,
It can actually be a productive joy
But not if no plan to the rushing,
And trying to fit everything into
Pressured time scales and dates,
That will ensure forms of panic
And restless and tired states.

Therefore you must slow it down
And allow time for a healthy cough,
But still uttering those desperate words
Please stop the world I want to get off.

For sometimes if any troubles come
It helps if we see what's going wrong,
Whilst that can be for many reasons
If worries go where they don't belong.

So an armistice or any short truce
Can help assimilate how you feel,
With some recollections and clarity
Of what was right and actually real,
Because in sad and emotional times
The exact facts can slip from sight,
So an armistice gives a good chance
To address wrongs and put them right.

--ooOoo--

Stretcher Bearers

It seems the world's no longer churning
And my treadmill has now stopped,
Which is a great and timely relief
For I fear that I may have dropped,
To the floor like some old rag doll
Who was no longer able to function,
Successfully and to a certain level
People saw will little compunction.

So I am enjoying some rest now
Because we must all have a break,
And this fact is so very important
To ensure we don't make a mistake,
Or perhaps clock off much too early
And that act really just won't do.
For there are judging eyes watching,
So keen to criticise me and you.

But if you put your hands up high
And say look at all that I have done,
Don't expect it to count with others
Even if their contribution was none,
For although all the propaganda says
We'll make sure you're not alone,
It doesn't seem to really work out
Even when you shout and moan.

Because there are none so deaf
As those who don't want to hear,
Just as the blindest person you ask
Won't see or come anywhere near.

Thus forgive me being knackered
For we can only give out so much,
While the accusing spectators of life
Remain silent and out of touch.

So best call for the stretcher bearers
To take another fatigued body away,
Because it's no further use now
And can't give another day!

--ooOoo--

Slipping Away

I can't reach you much anymore
You are just too far away,
And I know you're not understanding
Hardly anything I now say.

Though if I can keep it simple
It's still possible to get through,
But nothing like a conversation
Regarding things we used to do,
With all the places that we saw
And amazing experiences we had,
That now you can't remember
And that is so very sad.

An independence held so firm
Is now replaced by gross anxiety,
For you question every little task
That is now very hard to see.
Although there are fleeting bits
Of the person you once were,
For resistive and stubbornness stay
But so much is just a blur.

Thus we contemplate our years
And what will happen to us,
But should it be more adversity
We must confront it without fuss.
Though that is quite easy to say
For me who is so far unaffected,
By ageing pains and conditions
That have not with me connected.

But be sure any oncoming illnesses
Affecting my mind and health abilities,
Will be robustly resisted and fought
Before I go down on my knees.

--ooOoo--

Fragile Flame

The candle of life is very fragile
And suddenly you can lose the flame,
If the world turns you on your head
So that nothing now seems the same,
As you battle on with a futile fight
That was almost lost before the start,
But fading pride has coerced you here
With a desperation to play your part.

So weakly and without much hope
You protect the flickering spirit of light,
Praying that this tiny, fragile beacon
Doesn't die and leave you without sight.,
Because those intruding doubts and fears
Are more disturbingly scary in the dark,
So should you lose that little puny, glow
It can release all your fears, so stark.

Now as you recognise what's happening
Like biting off more than you can chew,
As you see now how your very best
Won't be near enough to save you,
From impending downfall of all you know
And that your accepted values are not true,
When you hear the raucous voices of doubt
Gathering large and loud to mock you.

Thus feel no disgrace as you now crumple
Beneath your heavy and crushing load,
You once believed that you could resist
Before more cruel burdens were bestowed,
Upon your unprotected and lonely soul
Now flinching and whimpering for peace,
From the bombardment all aimed at you
Which you despairingly see won't cease.

--ooOoo--

Out of Time

Not such a cheery poem this, but very important to me as it is about a very dear friend called Denise who was diagnosed with cancer and given two years to live, (which is actually what she had).

Denise had planned her "two years left" meticulously, putting everything in place for after her death. She did as much of her "list of things to do" things before her time ran out.

I was privileged to be with Denise just before she died, and at her funeral read out a eulogy she had asked me to write before she died. Quite a pressure, but at least I knew that she approved of my words for her. The poem also reflects the awful weather on the funeral day.

Crashing wind and driving rain
Really conspired to fill the day,
That you were finally laid to rest
And gave everyone their say,
Of all that you had meant to them
In each and every way.

But though your candle has gone out
Your spirit still shines bright,
And no disgusting weather's blast
Could cause us any doubt,
That you had brightened up the life
Of all that came in sight.

It's said that when you leave this earth
You wend your way to heaven,
But whether you believe in this
And however you are leaven,
None should have to leave the world
When they're aged just fifty seven!

Crashing winds and driving rain
Really conspired to fill the day,
That you were finally laid to rest
And made the light seem grey.
Crashing winds and driving rain
Washed the tears and gave it's sign,
That however hard you'd tried
You had still run out of time.

So now the final dye is cast
It is up to us to ponder,
Are we set for many better things
If in this life we squander,
Time and love that we may lose
Searching for a wide blue yonder.

--ooOoo--

A Closing of a Door

So you did get your final wish
To go to sleep and not awake,
But you were not always thus
With decisions like that to make.

For I remember a determined lady
With nothing allowed to get in the way.
Like walking paths you wanted to take,
Or jobs needing to be done that day.
So then it would be all systems go
As you tackled that particular chore,
Because I had very soon learnt
You would give your all, and more.

But there were many other times too
When we travelled round the globe,
To all those little tucked away places
You had determined we would probe.
Although we did also talk quite a lot
But I guess most of that was me,
When we sat and chatted over things
And did our very best to agree.

Sadly though that all came to an end
When cruel dementia took its grip,
To baffle your sharp, alert mind
And cause good reason to slip.

Thus choices you need to make now
I'm sure will be very hard to tell.
So I can only say goodbye then,
And R I P, and travel well.

--ooOoo--

I Won't Pass This Way Again

I have rambled and I have traipsed
Many places in both sun and rain,
But now I have made my decision
That I won't pass this way again.

For some places and situations
Seem more profound than the rest,
That often make decisions difficult
Like which are painful or the best.
For I have had my share of past upset
When I feared my soul might be slain,
So I determined it was time to go
And I won't pass this way again.

Because it seems sometimes in life
The more you give and harder you try,
It just might not all be good enough
However much you wonder why.
So I have shaken myself down hard
And am all prepared for the refrain,
For although I possibly might not lose
I still won't pass this way again.

So cast your stones and ready my cross
If I have been so drastically bad,
But I know that I did my very best
And that makes me feel quite sad.
For everyone fails sometimes in life
And maybe mine was despite my brain.
So goodbye even though I'm sure I won,
Because I won't pass this way again.

--ooOoo--

Laurie Wilkinson

Oh Happy Death?

Silently now the town hall clock
Looks downward on the streets to mock,
The world still alive, but almost dead
As the human race has lost the thread,
Of how to continue with any form
That can deal with a deadly virus storm,
Which has condemned everyday life
To a living death of depressive strife.

For basic interactions in a joyous crowd
Are now all banned and not allowed,
With streets silent in a deserted state
As for many now it's far too late
Having succumbed to an abrupt death
Strangled to take their final breath,
Before joining the fast growing list
Of casualties who will be sadly missed.

As little warning came of impending curse
From a virus determined to be the worst,
And prevent happy gatherings of love
Causing a living death or early trip above.

For in fact a half-life is now presiding
As many go with the Grim Reaper riding,
Claiming them from earths death knell
While we wait in solitude for our bell,
Calling departure from this mortal coil
As any happiness will drain in the soil.

So don't despair at your final loud ring
As we utter "Oh death where is thy sting?"
To release us from a world slowly dying
And save all futility of even trying,
To cope with a life of solitude spent
With no socialisation, fun or any content,
In lives that have seen a complete change
With only a future to be forever strange.

--ooOoo--

Ageing (Article)

The process of ageing is simply just becoming older. The term ageing refers particularly to human beings, many animals, and apparently fungi. I should say at this point that I take no responsibility for any possible downside repercussions for anyone reading this, and I will repeat, as a "reporting" poet, "as ever", my tongue may be in my cheek. I am just saying all this whilst safely sconced behind my "Poetic Licence".

For human beings, ageing represents the accumulation of changes over time, encompassing; physical mobility, general health, thinking, and social changes. Reaction time, for example, may slow with age, while knowledge of world events and wisdom may expand, but this is more likely down to life experiences and awareness.

Well that is what the definitions say, but more down to earth is the fact that most of the jokes, stories and humour about getting older, (we all laughed at when we were younger), sadly turn out to be true in later life. Not so funny then, and the only consolation is that everyone will get old no matter how hard we try. Many rich people, great leaders and in history, for example the Pharaohs with their pyramids, tried to stay young or have eternal youth or life, but nope, it doesn't happen!

All very grim, BUT it is our attitude and manner with which we deal with getting older that will mark our happiness and contentment with life. As I often say, you work it out and apply it in your own way, for I'm only a "fact presenting" (lol very young at heart) poet. To that end I have included more of my poems on ageing rather than text. Ignore at your peril!

Not That Kind of Time

With stealth and cruelty the years go by
Casting spells on both body and mind,
So that we wither and our frailties form
Thus we realise, time's not that kind.

Our resisting brain cells and lively wit
Dispute any damage is being done,
So you still believe you are fit and well
When in truth you can barely run!
But is it wrong to live a white lie?
You're still young and everything works,
For the real truth will slowly seep in
So that doubts and uncertainty lurks.

Going back over time, you now see it all.
The things you did, or should have tried,
For however much you want to catch up
You can't do this when you've died!

The march of the years won't be stopped
Whatever actions you try to pursue.
For once you did things to kill time,
But that time is now killing you!

With stealth and cruelty the years go by
Casting spells on both body and mind,
So that we wither and our frailties form
Thus we realise, time's not that kind.

They say time and tides wait for no man
Though we can do things as they release,
But do not squander or spoil the years
Or you will lose your inner peace.
So maybe best to make a covenant now
As your body loses all strength and vigour,
For the secret of youth and endless life
Is a solution we are yet to figure!

--ooOoo—

That poem is from my 3rd book, and perhaps take note,
it's just "killing time, when it is now killing you?" Not
you obviously, or is it? Don't worry for I have included
a "smile" poem, but NO cheating!

I give you my own perspective now in the following
poem, which is published in my fourth book Life Scene
in Verse.

Alone in the Mirror

I am alone in the mirror
With this face I've come to know,
That's been staring back at me
From so many years ago.
But that face has changed now
Though the expression is the same,
For it has seen much of life
And situations you can't tame.

This face has looked on loss
So tragic it creased with pain,
While trying hard to smile out
As inside the heart was slain.
Inner traumas rocked the soul
Which nearly split the seam.
Causing untold agony but,
Outside the face would beam.

So laughter which we cherish
Has cracked the outer look,
Though these smile fed lines
Will belie the times it shook,
With mirth, and sometimes grief
As it was worn across the years,
That eroded pristine youth
With many of life's fears.

So that cruel mirror on my wall
Reflects the good and bad,
Showing with lines and wrinkles
All the years of life I've had.
But I'm not ashamed of this
Please don't be taken in.
For though sometimes I force it,
Years drop off when I grin.

--ooOoo—

You may take note of my "little hint" at the end, but totally up to you... I will be watching!

Of course much of getting older can be hard to deal with. For example, the need to get to a loo faster but with a less swift body! However it is our fortitude and probably how we deal with it all that really matters. Some more hits in next poem.

Sticks and Frames

However sturdy was your prime
In old age you're not the same,
For many a fit and healthy man
Now has to use a stick or frame.

Even worse if you let things go
In matters of your future health,
Smoking and gross indulgence
Will certainly help age's stealth,
As it creeps up steadily in time
Quicker the less exercise you do.
For often when it comes to life
Most decisions are down to you.

Pretending you're too tired or ill
For any activity or a game,
Will surely accelerate the need
To use a walking stick or frame.

Sitting for hours inert in a chair
When you can move about much more,
Allows our bodies to slow down
Though of that you won't be sure.
So makes excuses as you will
That you're unlucky and not to blame,
If misfortune should condemn you
To have a stick or walking frame.

But whether any of this is true
And should you hide from any shame,
Maybe it would have taken longer
To require your stick or walking frame.

--ooOoo—

All jolly stuff then, so, "gird your loins" and make the most of good times! You always do, right? Great, nothing much to worry about then...

Backing Down

Lengthening shadows slowly creep
And impose more upon your years,
For this is the way it's been decreed
And brings about our fears,
That we can't cope any more
At the mercy of deaths sting,
Which has people on their knees
And scary nightmares bring.

So our very table of substances
Now allows us all to exist,
But should these be taken away
Their very presence may be missed.
For in many people's situation
Life's changes can take from them,
All the power of independence
Whilst constant pain will condemn.

Thus creeping about the world
Accumulated years take their toll,
Leaving hollow wrecks of folk
Who used to jig and rock and roll,
Along with other vibrant methods
That would depict life in a dance.
But now with the passing of time
For them existence is a trance.

But do not fear or be ashamed
Of those marching years you feel,
For however rich or famous
Life will continue to deal
Out the same sad treatment
To everybody, one and all.
However hard that it hits home
We must accept a dignified appal.

--ooOoo—

All spelt out then, but nothing we didn't know or were aware of, although some may have wasted their time or years? I can only just reiterate that we must count our blessings and enjoy our time as much as possible!

--ooOoo—

Dying Breathes

Another day in a sort of living death
So you briefly wonder about taking breath,
To absorb and fight on another bland day
Like a child with their toys taken away.

For there are no excitements as before,
The thrill of a race, or what's the score?
No social gatherings for a laugh or a joke
As pub and cafe closures start to choke,
Your beliefs in, or a fear of Covid 19
This silent killer so menacing and mean,
Sweeping in as some invisible tsunami
And making our whole world go barmy.

For there's no normal life or apparent reason
To existing in an eternally dark, winter season,
With this constant eerie silence and deep fear
Of anything arriving or even coming near.

Thus a vast, psychotic paranoia now presides
With very little chance of leaving insides,
To where we have all been banished to serve
A suffocating sentence we didn't deserve.

So say your prayers to any god or cause
Hoping for their mercy or even to pause,
An overwhelming depressive, restrictive state
Controlling thoughts and world with no date,
Of any relief from this actual hell on earth
Making us wish we'd not been given a birth.
As we buckle in our seats, and gird our loins,
For a ride no more certain than tossing coins.

For we are in unprecedented times and days
With everyone pleading that it no longer stays.
This horrid curse that's never before been seen,
Presenting as a Devil's work called Covid 19.

--ooOoo--

Lessons to be Learnt

Your country needs you the posters said
And you can fight beside your chums,
So off they went to the war in France
And said goodbye to girls and mums.

Very ordinary chaps, not heroes yet
Were all excited, feeling hearts soar,
Marching off to their great adventure
To win a war that will end all war.

Well that was the propaganda then
And may even have been said in fear,
For sadly that was not to happen
At any time after, or in a future year.
Because the unprecedented bloodbath
Caused mass suffering and deprivation,
As world war one's attrition dragged on
With atrocities that stunned a nation.

So men who were totally unprepared
Witnessed sights that shouldn't be seen,
Like petrified men drowning in mud,
Gassed, or blown up in deaths obscene.
Thus casualty figures hardly believable
Rose as the slaughter went on unabated.
For that final push was regularly tried
On wasted, bloody ground not sated.

With thousands of men mowed down
Strewn in agony or a hideous death,
Many crucified across the barbed wire
As devils disciples gasped for breath,
While their evil work was continued
But performed by unknowing men,
Who had only answered a patriotic call
That took them to hell there and then.

And so agonising slaughter continued
By new weaponry invented to kill,
Flowers of a generation sent to solve
Arguments that war never will.

--ooOoo--

The Pool and the Leaves

There's a camp site by my French place
With a small, round swimming pool,
That gets leaves dropping in it
Which is not too good at all.
So every morning of each day
The site manager would get them out.
Which was appreciated by swimmers,
And of that there is no doubt.

He also used to maintain the camp
Making sure everything was clean,
Not just because it was his job
But so it looked nice when seen.
Though sadly he is no longer here
For cruel cancer took him away,
And those leaves are still dropping
But the pool gets cleared each day.

So as I pass, or sit with a drink
At the site bar that's just nearby,
I often get to wonder about life
Which can often make us cry.
For the man who cleaned the pool
Was nowhere near my years,
Yet was removed from life early
Condemning his family to tears.

Now many of us will leave things
That occupy ourselves and time,
And when we have left the world
We hope memories remain sublime.
So for me it's my words and poems
About love, life and she who grieves,
Over things still here without us
Like the man who cleared the leaves.

--ooOoo--

Lambs and Guns

I wrote this in disgust at a terrorist attack on innocent people mostly on beaches and surrounding area in Tunisia about 2016. The cowardly attack was one of a recent spate around that time, and I vented my feelings in this poem.

These words are also very well received when I read it at my poetry gigs, (when it is appropriate as my readings are mostly humorous, reflective and upbeat), but one must cut cards with the devil at times. Hold on tight....

I am naked except for my clothes
No match for knives, bombs and gun.
You can kill me anytime you want
For my only defence is to run.

You are fully armed to your teeth
A veritable arsenal moving on legs,
So you can slaughter and maim at will
No matter how much your victim begs,
As they relax, carefree on a beach,
At a cafe, or maybe a music hall.
Thus your foul war on the unarmed
Ensures that only the innocents fall!

Creeping, slithering, making your plans
Hiding in shadows behind a locked door.
Disgusting cowards, strapping on bombs
For your sick, ambushing war.

Thus you avoid, and won't bring to combat
Any trained and well-armed man.
So you stick to putrid sewers,
And attack like only scum can.

For I am naked except for my clothes
No match against knife, bombs and gun.
You can try to kill me anytime you want,
But it's not my only defence, to run.

So stalk our free world, trying to see
Easy targets like lambs, unaware at play,
Your brainwashed mind and smoking gun
Will never earn a winners sway.

--ooOoo--

Ted & Beth's Sadness

Ted and Beth miss their human mum
Who passed away a few months ago,
For they have told me of their sadness
Asking me to pen some words, and so
I have put together this poem for them,
Remembering times they had enjoyed,
With various activities and travels shared
As their fun and mischief they employed.

They recall their mum playing the piano
Both for them and at my poem reading gigs,
Where she sometimes helped entertain folks
That enjoyed the poems, bears and little jigs,
Sitting in their chairs and listening to it all
And often joining in as best they could.
But however much that they all managed
We remember it as being very good.

Now Ted remembers in his early years
Coming with us down the Amazon River,
That he recalls with great excitement
And also met a Tapir that made him quiver,
But it was very friendly, and all was well.
For not long after he and Beth were united
Spending time together travelling with us,
While sharing their bears love so requited.

They then stayed with us in our little tent
Going round Australia and many other places,
But often had to travel in the plane holds
So they would have no drug check traces,
Which they understood but didn't like
Being relieved when journeys were done,
That included time at our French home
Out in our dinghy they thought great fun.

So the bears have many happy memories
Of times spent with their human mum,
Who they knew hadn't been too well
But didn't expect the end would come
So quickly as it was to all turn out
Although they had still talked to her,
Which gives them nice warm memories
In both of their hearts and fur.

--ooOoo--

Am I Dead?

I guess I must be dead now
For I feel no pain, or a life.
And nothing touches me
To bring succour or more strife.
And I can't see outside my box
That's how confinement feels.
Locked in consuming darkness
Which my personality steals.

I look out with sightless eyes
Upon a blackness staring back,
Into my empty, void-like brain
That feels it must now crack,
From all this unseen pressure
Pushing me helpless to the ground.
And even if I can get up again,
No sanctuary will be found.

So am I dead then, I must ask?
But only echoes answer now,
For nothing outside gets in
As nobody will know how.
So then I must be dead
Trapped in my limbo state,
Suffocated and being crushed
By an entity I now hate.

Although a flicker of some hope
I may escape from my regression.
When hearing daunting words say,
I'm suffering from depression!

--ooOoo--

Easy in the End

I've been very lucky with my health
And people say I don't look my years,
But maybe I'm a very good actor
So can always hide my tears.

Because we will all cry at something
Perhaps some injustice in our lives,
For however hard you try for honesty
Somebody always spreads some lies,
Which can really bring us down
Especially if feeling we're all alone,
For it's easy to be big in a crowd
But in solitude harder to atone.

So when treading a lonely road
Even if surrounded by a throng,
Who seem to appreciate you
Giving out laughter and a song,
But inside you may be aching
To shout out about how you feel,
But it will often fall on deaf ears
Or be disbelieved as just not real.

But I can't have any complaints
As I've trod the world far and wide,
With more laughter than sorrow
Though often having sadness inside.
For each and every single one of us
No matter how hard you try to deny,
Will have nagging doubts in you
And constant questions of why?

So best to sit and make a covenant
You can rest easy with until the end.
Because if I have learnt just one thing,
Doubt can drive you round the bend.

Though I'm not too scared of dying
And on that I am completely sure,
For I'll make certain I'm not dangling
Too long over the world's exit door.

--ooOoo--

Appendix

Kind compliments and feedback to me on my poetry increases as I continue to write and produce more books, number nine now, but it still recounts that many people like to work out the meanings of my poems for themselves, or even attach their own personal experiences and thoughts as they resonate with them. I think that is truly wonderful, but for other folks who like to seek my reasons and explanations for them my poems, please review my comments below.

As I tend to write spontaneously and often on subjects that have really emoted me, I will mostly "nail my thoughts in". Most of the themes are quite clear or self-explanatory, however, the poems listed in this appendix below are the less obvious topics and thoughts. Please feel free to attach any personalisation or special meaning that they have for you individually, because I will feel really honoured if you do!

Love and Trees:
An abstract poem showing how we can take things for granted and even stop noticing and appreciating them.

Left Turn Loons:
On selfish and thoughtless drivers, particularly those not using indicators

Ode To Sylvie's Ears:

In a very hot spell Sylvie the presenter mentioned on air that her headphones were making her ears sweat! This poem that I later read on BBC Radio Sussex & Surrey was the result. Sylvie a great sport, "loved it".

Fore Fathers:

My poetic tribute to fathers requested by Sylvie Blackmore for her show after I read out my poem for mums on Mothering Sunday. I read this poem out live too.

You Can't Wear Your Hat In Here:

Fairly obvious from the poem, but is more on my being incredulous at request, or more a demand, to remove my cap.

A Knock Upon My Door:

My thoughts for all carers after I had a demanding caring role thrust on me.

Questioning Fete:

My take on an "oft asked question", but maybe pointing out the times that we feel and ask the question?

Figment:
Some suggestions and perhaps explanations of how minds can work in expansive manner at times, often when stressed, and some insight into my vivid imagination and inspirations.

Born Anew:
The recognition of times in our life when we have to, or consider a clean and fresh start. My recent experiences are touched on to hopefully help others.

Beam:
Recognising that at times, usually the difficult ones, a good friend, special person or belief can help you get by.

Armistice:
My reminder that we all need, or should take some time out, to reflect on things, reconsider, and even if don't make changes, at least have a break.

Stretcher Bearers:
My shout out that many people caring or supporting others need help too, and while this purported help is readily talked about as being available and there, in reality it isn't, and very rarely happens or is given, thus the carers often drop.

Fragile Flame:
That you must find the will to continue no matter how much life and people continue to load onto you, but recognising that there is only so much one person can do.

A Closing of a Door:
Poem I wrote about my wife and for her funeral service in March 2021.

I Won't Pass This Way Again:
On finally making a decision that a person, place or situation is impossible and you cannot ever win with, even if it's not your fault, so you give up on it.

Oh Happy Death:
On living only half a life with no fun as initially caused by Coronavirus, but for some people this is sadly their norm?

Dying Breathes:
The consuming effect of Covid 19 when first arriving and condemning us all to a barren world of boredom and often solitude.

Lambs and Guns:
Another of my poems published after reaching national finals, and written in disgust at the Paris terror atrocity November 2015.

Easy in the End:
Describes contemplating our future life at some of our lowest times and considering how we will make a pact with ourselves for future thoughts and feelings.

More?

I hope that you enjoyed this book
For I tried to pack lots in,
With various themes in sections
So you can choose where to begin,
And take yourself on journeys
Or if you wished to, just remain.
For I have other books out now,
Thus you can have it all again.

With poems to make you romantic
And some verses if you feel deep.
Others will make you look back on life,
Even smile when you go to sleep.

Of course Ted and Beth will feature
I can hardly leave them out.
As surely they'll have new adventures,
Well of this I have no doubt!
And I will have new observations
I glean from scanning life's tree.
Take care then you are not included
When I write down what I see.

So please look at my other books
And support "Help for Heroes" too,
For all my sales donate to them
From my poems I write for you.

You can get books from my website online
And to message me direct will be fine.
With every contact listed below
Including all that you need to know,
To search for me on the Amazon club
Or just come and find me down the pub!

My other books are:-
Poetic Views of Life
MORe Poetic Views of Life
Reviews of Life in Verse
Life Scene in Verse
Life Presented in Verse
Poet Reveals All
Poet Reflects Your World
Poetic Seeds to Fruition

My contacts:-
Email = lw1800@hotmail.co.uk
Amazon authors page= Laurie Wilkinson
Facebook page = The Psychy Poet Laurie Wilkinson
Facebook page =Ted n Beth of Laurie the Poet
Website = www.lauriewilkinson.com

Printed in Great Britain
by Amazon